What To Do When Your Partner Has
Diabetes:
A Survival Guide

by

Nicole Johnson, DrPH, MPH, MA
Miss America 1999
Living With Type 1 Diabetes Since 1993

&

Lorraine Stiehl
Diabetes Advocate
Partner of a Loved One With Diabetes Since 1985

WHAT TO DO WHEN YOUR PARTNER HAS DIABETES:
A SURVIVAL GUIDE

by
Nicole Johnson, DrPH, MPH, MA
Living with Type 1 Diabetes Since 1993
&
Lorraine Stiehl
Partner of a Loved One With Diabetes Since 1985

CONTRIBUTORS
Stephanie Melton, PhD, MPH, MA
Chris Stiehl, Living with Type 1 Diabetes Since 1960

*"Type 1 diabetes can often be overwhelming not only
for those affected but also for their spouses and families.
Nicole Johnson provides a wonderful and practical,
easy to read and 'must have' book for all those
supporting a partner with Type 1 diabetes."*

DR. DES SCHATZ
Professor & Associate Chair of Pediatrics, Medical Director,
Diabetes Center, University of Florida College of Medicine,
Past President, American Diabetes Association 2016

Special thanks to my dear husband, Chris, who I appreciate so much.
He has helped me to be the person I am today. I am grateful
to him for his tremendous support of me personally,
and for his tenacity in fighting this challenging disease.
He is my hero, my Clark Kent, my Superman. I love you, Chris.

LORRAINE STIEHL

To my daughter Ava, may you learn about the value
of relationship through these stories of tenderness
and compassion. You are the greatest diabetes partner
your Mom could ever ask for! I love you!

NICOLE JOHNSON

CONTENTS

FOREWORD

A FAMILY PARTNERSHIP

John and I have been honored to know Nicole Johnson since she was first named Miss America 1999. We have also known Lorraine Stiehl through her work in diabetes with JDRF so we welcomed the opportunity to help fill an unmet need. This book is truly unique and so very necessary.

When John was diagnosed at the age of 6 in the early 1940s, doctors told his mother he wouldn't live past 15 or 20. At that time, there was no way to measure blood sugar, the quality of insulin was a lot different, and the needles were huge. It was tough.

As an adult, John welcomed new treatments and therapies including improved insulin, home blood sugar testing, and disposable needles that made his day-to-day care a little easier. When John reflects on his early life with diabetes, he remembers never thinking much about what "could be" until our daughter, Allison, was diagnosed with T1D when she was 25.

Seeing our daughter struggle with diabetes brought about all kinds of feelings of guilt and sadness to us. We knew that John must manage his diabetes even more meticulously in order to help Allison manage hers. I became our CEO (Chief Emotional Officer) and played a really critical role for both of them.

Although Allison and John were diagnosed 40 years apart, they essentially began testing their blood at the same time, as the first personal glucose meters did not become available until the early '80s. It was technology and the strength of our family partnership that made all of the difference in our ability to survive and thrive with diabetes.

Here are our collective words of wisdom from over 100 years of living with this challenging disease:

- Never be embarrassed about having diabetes—just tell people what they have to do to help you manage it;

- Take advantage of the technology to manage your diabetes;

- Don't complain about having diabetes—get involved in working for a cure;

- Share this book with everyone you know.

All the best,

Marilyn, John and Allison

Marilyn, John and Allison

John and Marilyn McDonough have been married for 60 years and have five children and eight grandchildren. John is the Co-Founder and Chairman of McDonough Medical Products Corporation. He has served on many Boards, including as Chairman, Board of Directors of the Juvenile Diabetes Research Foundation (JDRF) International and, is a Life Member of JDRF's Illinois Chapter. He and Marilyn founded JDRF's Florida Suncoast Chapter's Annual Hope Gala and The McDonough Family Foundation has provided millions of dollars for T1D research.

Allison McDonough Lascelle has served as a role model to countless volunteers through her leadership positions on the Juvenile Diabetes Research Foundation International's Lay Review Research Committee, was named Person of the Year by JDRF's Illinois Chapter, and has testified along with her Dad at a Senate Hearing on behalf of JDRF's Children's Congress in Washington, D.C.

INTRODUCTION

———————————·❧·———————————

This is a practical guide for anyone loving and living with diabetes in your relationship. You will learn about the good, bad and ugly parts of this disease and what it can do to relationships. This book tackles the overriding themes that impact everything in your relationship including disease unpredictability, frustration, control issues and fear.

Inside you will find quotes from people who have successfully walked down the pathway of life with diabetes with their partner. After reading this book, you will feel comforted knowing you are not alone. In the end, diabetes can help strengthen you and the relationship you have with your partner.

WHAT THE SCIENTIFIC RESEARCH LITERATURE SAYS

It is no surprise partners play a key role in supporting diabetes management. Diabetes management doesn't happen alone. Diabetes affects not only your family's daily life, but also how you interact with your loved one. Research shows that family members play a key role in helping with diabetes management.[1,2] In fact, better family functioning is associated with improved diabetes management and glucose control.[3] On the next few pages, we will share some key research findings to learn from and enhance your interactions with your partner with diabetes.

THE ROLE OF PARTNERS

One of the important issues partners face is knowing how to help their loved one in useful ways. For couples living with diabetes, a key distinction is between social control and caregiving. Social control involves directly using pressure to change behavior.[4] Sometimes this can be necessary in emergency situations, but trying to control behavior daily can backfire and be interpreted as nagging or criticism by your partner with diabetes. If this happens, partners with diabetes may resist by hiding unhealthy behaviors, ignoring requests or deliberately engaging in unhealthy behaviors.[5] They may also feel that you are questioning their independence and ability to take care of themselves.

Understanding how we give support and show care is useful for avoiding ineffective, controlling behavior. Different ways of giving support have been identified as:[6]

- Emotional support (showing care, love and empathy)

- Appraisal support (providing feedback on their behavior or critiquing)

- Informational support (giving suggestions and information to help problem solve)

- Instrumental support (proving direct assistance with self-care tasks like picking up a prescription)

Brenda Jean Bailey and Arlene Kahn[7] found that all of the above forms of support were generally appreciated by individuals with diabetes, except appraisal support, which was described as feeling like judgments of their behavior. For example, when questioned about a late insulin injection or missing a meal with a negative verbal tone and body language, the person with diabetes can feel criticized. In this way even well-intentioned reminders can feel like nagging. This is especially true if the person with diabetes felt like the reminder wasn't needed. Individuals with diabetes also reported responding more appreciatively to help when they felt like their partners were genuinely concerned for their well being without judgment. Paula Trief and colleagues found that perceptions of help differed by gender.[8] In their research of couples affected by diabetes, men noticed and reported more instrumental support, while women talked more about verbal support and encouragement.

This highlights a key issue that people with diabetes want to feel respected and trusted to take care of themselves. In a study conducted by Nicole Johnson and Stephanie Melton, when partners described trusting their loved ones' capability for self-care, partners reported feeling less need to be involved directly in diabetes care or nag.[9] They took on a supportive role by providing emotional and instrumental support. However, if a health crisis occurred, or if their partner was experiencing diabetes burnout, they helped more with daily diabetes management.

Understanding how to help appropriately can mean less stress and fewer tense interactions in your relationship. An area that can be ripe for conflict is food. In a study by Melissa Franks and colleagues, among older couples living with type 2 diabetes, those with diabetes who reported receiving more encouragement to eat healthier and who also shared more meals with their partner reported less diabetes distress.[10] The authors found that partners who tried to control what their loved one ate or critiqued them for unhealthy food choices had higher levels of stress related to diabetes. Further, positive reinforcement of healthy diet choices, such as congratulating when they made a healthy food choice, was associated with better blood sugar control and overall diabetes management than critiquing unhealthy food choices.

This is good news! Becoming more aware of how you interact and softening your approach in interactions may not only improve your relationship, but also may positively affect how well your partner copes with diabetes.

The research literature shows that whether attempts to help will be met with gratitude or resistance depend on if the person with diabetes feels they need help and what they believe their partner's motivations are.[7] The lesson is that when we approach diabetes management with compassion, we all do better. Negotiating how to give support begins with conversations about what your partner needs and how you can best help them.

PARTNER ADVICE

Conversation Starters to Navigate the Support Role

"How much help do you want or need?"

"When I do [x], it is in an effort to be supportive of all the things you have to deal with as it relates to diabetes. Is this a help to you, or a frustration?"

"Am I trying to give you enough or too much help?"

"How does it feel for you when I try to help?"

"What am I doing now that is working that I could do more of?"

HOW DIABETES AFFECTS PARTNERS

Your partner may be very independent with their diabetes, or perhaps they ask for a little more help. Regardless, to some degree you provide caregiving to your loved one. Research shows that the additional worry partners feel can take a toll on the them as caregivers.[9,11] Partners describe helping with meal planning or preparation, or carrying emergency food in case of a low blood sugar. Partners can feel that they have to help care for their loved ones, especially if the person with diabetes requests it.[12] This can lead to feeling burdened. Diabetes becomes one more thing the partner must handle besides their own personal responsibilities. It takes time and energy to provide support like shopping for different foods, or timing meals. Chances are you may also consciously or subconsciously watch your loved one for signs of low blood sugar. You may feel the need to ask them how they are feeling or worry about making sure they have enough insulin and supplies on hand. All of these small worries can add up to increase your burden. Psychologists call this diabetes distress, or the daily stresses that accumulate over time to make you feel worried and overwhelmed.[13] Distress is different from depression, which often interferes with daily functioning. Depression may be more common among people with diabetes, and you should be aware of the signs of depression for you and your partner.[10] Distress in those with diabetes and in their partners is associated with poorer diabetes control and lower relationship satisfaction. These are important reasons to lessen the stress of living with diabetes as much as possible.

The literature shows us that the burden partners can feel depends on how effectively the person with diabetes is managing the condition and engaging in healthy behaviors.[5]

HOW DIABETES IMPACTS RELATIONSHIPS

The stress that comes from living with diabetes can take a toll on relationships. Daily challenges, such as handling low blood sugars, figuring out how to use or troubleshoot diabetes technology like continuous glucose monitors (CGM), and negotiating how or if blood sugar numbers are shared between partners, can all add issues to your relationship.[14,15] Diabetes can become the third partner in a relationship and so it is beneficial to maintain open communication. Trief and colleagues have found that couples' beliefs about the quality of their relationships, and how close they felt to their partner were associated with blood sugar control.[16] Struggles with diabetes management can spill over into daily interactions and intimacy, thus affecting the quality of life for couples. As we have pointed out interactions around diabetes can increase conflict. Unfortunately, negative social interaction can have a greater impact on a relationship than positive exchanges.[17] Therefore, partners may interpret negative reactions more harshly when couples are experiencing a rough patch.

This means that a few negative conflicts can weigh down a marriage or partnership significantly, and couples need more positive, loving moments to outweigh them. In the following chapters we present insights on topics that can lead to conflict between partners, and provide you with ideas to lessen stress and conflict with your loved one.

This book has been designed to be a quick read for you, the partner of a loved one living with diabetes.

 If you wish to hear from other partners on how they manage their relationship with diabetes, read the text boxes labeled **PARTNER PERSPECTIVE**. Sixteen partners have shared their experiences in this book.

 If you seek helpful tips from other partners, look at the **PARTNER ADVICE** boxes. These are designed to be practical, quick tips for you to incorporate into your life.

Even though this book has been written for the partners of those with type 1 diabetes, there is helpful information for those who have partners with type 2 diabetes. As you will see throughout the book, it is all about communication.

CHAPTER ONE

Love and Life with Diabetes

You seek companionship. A life partner. You meet someone and feel a special chemistry. Your relationship moves forward. Then, at some point, you find out there is a third partner in your relationship: type 1 diabetes. It is like a three-legged stool. You soon realize that if one part of the stool breaks everything comes shattering down. Diabetes is complicated and if not cared for properly can negatively affect every part of your lives together, but if approached with compassion it can also bring you both great opportunity.

LORRAINE

"In the mid-1980s, I met a man who would change my life in many ways. Not only was I attracted to him because of his passion, compassion and intellect (and the fact that he reminded me of Clark Kent!), I loved that we had so much in common and he could make me laugh.

After a half dozen dates, I remember when a syringe and vial came out of hiding. I remember watching the first injection and thinking, "He either has diabetes or he does drugs." Since I had an aunt, cousin and classmate with type 1 diabetes, I realized that the vial looked like an insulin bottle. From that moment on I knew that diabetes would be the third partner in our relationship.

My husband and I have had an amazing relationship for over 30 years. He is my soul mate. However, like all partners, we have experienced high points in our relationship—and low points. Diabetes has not made things easy. We have been angered and frustrated by this disease, and scared. We've been challenged by tremendous physical, mental and emotional obstacles. Thankfully, we've powered through it all—together. We are both stronger—and closer—because of his disease.

In the mid-1980s, diabetes management was difficult. We used to crudely check my husband's blood sugar by comparing colors on a test strip with the colors on the bottle of strips. A few years into our marriage, I figured out that my husband was color blind and yet that was how he managed diabetes for years!

Back then, we were "flying blind." My husband's diabetes management was unpredictable and stressful. As a newlywed, I remember crying in the middle of the night after a severe low blood sugar, wondering how I was going to keep my husband alive.

Thankfully, diabetes management tools improved. I remember when my husband brought home his first blood sugar meter. It took five minutes and there were many steps involved—but at least it worked. Soon after, my husband shared the results of a new diagnostic test called a hemoglobin A1c test. We were skeptical at first. How could one test assess blood sugar levels over a three-month period? Who would have guessed this test would still be in use today? And, of course, it was wonderful the day that my husband brought home human insulin and no longer had to rely on beef and pork insulin that discolored his skin and caused so many other problems.

Even though innovation in diabetes care continued to bring us great new tools such as insulin pumps and continuous glucose (sugar) monitors, the nearly three decades of "flying blind" took their toll on my husband. Together, we experienced almost every diabetes complication imaginable. There were a few times that I almost lost him. Thankfully, we were able to get through those dark days. Our love for each other—plus humor (important in any relationship!)—helped us to survive.

My husband and I have become stronger and more resilient through our involvement in diabetes non-profit organizations including the Juvenile Diabetes Research Foundation (JDRF). Two years after we were married, I became the third chapter staff member in the country to be hired by JDRF. After 14 years as a local, regional and national staff member, I became an active volunteer for JDRF. Through our more than 30 years with JDRF, my husband and I have met so many families struggling to manage diabetes—and so many partners whose relationships have been challenged.

For decades, I have thought about how much a resource would have helped me in my relationship with my husband and diabetes. At one point I wished to write a book called, "Hunky Firemen in the Bedroom: The Ups & Downs of Having a Partner with Type 1 Diabetes." Thanks to life-changing technological advances in diabetes, I haven't needed our local paramedics as often as I once did!

What I would have given for this kind of book 30 years ago!"

≈≈≈

DIABETES ESSENTIALS

Let's cover a few basics starting with the definition of diabetes. Type 1 Diabetes (T1D) is an autoimmune disease that destroys insulin-producing beta cells in the pancreas. Both genetic factors and environmental triggers are involved in the onset of the disease. T1D has nothing to do with diet or lifestyle. Even though diabetes management tools have improved, there is still no cure for this disease.

Approximately 5 percent of all people with diabetes have T1D, approximately 1.45 million Americans.[18]

T1D is not a death sentence. Major advances in treatment in the past 30 years have extended life expectancy to match the life expectancy of those not living with T1D.

Type 2 diabetes (T2D) affects the majority of people with diabetes in the world. In T2D, the body does not use insulin properly. This is called insulin resistance. At first, the pancreas makes extra insulin to make up for the metabolic challenges present, but over time the pancreas isn't able to keep up and can't make enough insulin to keep blood sugar levels normal. T2D is treated with lifestyle changes, oral medications (pills) and insulin.

Insulin is critical to surviving T1D. It is a hormone produced in the pancreas (for those who do not have T1D) that controls the level of sugar in the blood. Insulin permits cells to use sugar (or glucose) for energy. Insulin, for a person with diabetes, can be delivered in a variety of ways—syringe, pen, pump or inhaler.

There are many other medications that might be a part of your loved one's disease management. These are all determined in concert with a health professional. Medications are aimed at helping the person with diabetes gain near normal blood sugar levels, or prevent or manage complications that have been caused by elevated blood sugar.

Near normal blood sugar control significantly reduces the risk of developing complications and prevents complications from getting worse—in both types of diabetes. There is hope and a great life can happen with diabetes. It all hinges on blood sugar control.

PARTNER ADVICE

Remain calm and don't panic during your partner's high or low blood sugars. Educate yourself on what to do when your partner requires assistance.

Your partner's A1c test (also known as hemoglobin A1c, HbA1c, or glyco-hemoglobin test) provides information about average blood sugar levels over the past 3 months. The most important thing to remember is that this value is a number, not a judgment. The number can serve as motivation and lead your partner toward setting goals. You can be a part of these goals, just avoid any judgment or preconceived notions about what you think will or will not work. The goals have to be decided upon by the person with diabetes because that person must completely believe in the usefulness, potential and merit of the goals. To achieve goals, you must first believe in them.

Life with diabetes is like a science experiment. It can be messy, painful and tedious. It is important to remember the stress that accompanies this kind of constant disease management. Your partner with diabetes may celebrate the journey or may walk a path of disguise and hurt. It is up to you to determine the best way to walk alongside of the person you love. Supportive, loving care is a building block toward positive health. You can do this—together!

PARTNER PERSPECTIVE

"Understand how complicated diabetes is—and how many variables are in play, and the juggling act it requires of your partner each day. Patience and love is so very important."

PARTNER OF SOMEONE WITH T1D

NICOLE

"My diabetes is frustrating the majority of the time. By remembering that I am constantly beating myself up for small failures in my day-to-day care, my partner has a better sense of how to help me resolve my personal doubts and get past road blocks. This kind of loving support and encouragement helps me move forward and is very effective."

CHAPTER TWO

The Relationship Balancing Act

In all relationships, success often comes down to how well the couple balances their love life with everything else in their lives—work, school, family, friends, recreational activities, etc. T1D can certainly complicate all aspects of your life.

Most of the time, your partner with T1D will prefer to independently manage his/her own disease, and will not seek constant support from you or others. However, due to the nature of diabetes, it is often necessary for you to engage— especially if low blood sugar episodes are involved. Sometimes you must take full control of the situation until your partner recovers from his/her impaired state. How you handle taking control in these types of situations, and how you ultimately relinquish control, is important for your overall relationship success.

PARTNER PERSPECTIVE

"When my partner is semi-conscious due to a low blood sugar, I often ask him to say my name. Once he can do so, I know he is OK. When he starts talking in complete sentences, I know he is back in control—and I can relax."

PARTNER OF SOMEONE WITH T1D

When you are in a relationship with a partner with T1D, it is natural to question your partner's self-care. You may have specific concerns about what and when your partner eats, how and when your partner exercises, and even the amount of insulin he or she is taking.

PARTNER PERSPECTIVE

"Timing is everything. Make sure you understand when and where your partner feels the most comfortable having you ask health-related questions."

PARTNER OF SOMEONE WITH T1D

How you approach your partner as it relates to questions or concerns you have about his or her diabetes is critical. Make sure you aren't judgmental or appear to be nagging. Be aware that what you say may be interpreted negatively by your partner. Think about how you would respond being asked or spoken to in the manner you are using. Also, avoid being parental to your partner. Your partner may have emotional scars from early life with diabetes that this kind of approach or perceived behavior could irritate.

Consider that while we feel it is our prerogative to know our partner's blood sugar level, or what he or she is doing to manage diabetes, it may not—in that particular moment—be what is good for our partner. Like with so many aspects of relationships, there is a give and take; there are moments that seem unfair. Our motivations are right, but we, as partners, should be careful to avoid feeling it is necessary to insert ourselves just because we have concerns. Timing conversations about health-related issues carefully can mean the difference between getting shut out and having productive communication.

PARTNER ADVICE

Figure out how to support your partner without micromanaging (backseat driving).

MANAGING CONFLICT

All relationships have some degree of conflict—it is to be expected. Determining how you know when you are having relationship challenges versus diabetes challenges can be difficult.

It is important to figure out how you and your partner handle your differences, whether they are due to the relationship or due to diabetes. Well-managed conflict can be positive in bringing issues out in the open and making your relationship stronger.

Psychologist John Gottman and colleagues[19] teach about conflict management through the description of four behaviors that can destroy any relationship.

1. CRITICISM (Criticism is the expression of disapproval or the analysis and judgment of merits or faults.)

2. CONTEMPT (Contempt is showing disgust or hostility by mocking, sarcasm or name-calling.)

3. DEFENSIVENESS (Defensiveness is the display of behavior intended to divert blame.)

4. STONEWALLING (Stonewalling is a persistent refusal to communicate or to express emotions.)

Avoid these tempting behaviors to have the best results in conflict resolution. If not avoided, a cycle of negativity can result that may lead to emotion overload and a downward spiral of distrust and isolation.

There are some techniques that can ease dangerous and emotionally charged conversations and conflict. These techniques include:

1. Using a gentle conversation start up ("I feel" instead of "You did.")

2. Taking responsibility for your actions ("You are right. I want to do better at that.")

3. Showing appreciation to each other ("Remember how we used to…" or "I loved when we used to…")

4. Soothing yourself and each other to decrease tension related to your negative emotions (take a walk, breathe deeply, listen to music, etc.)

For your relationship to flourish, it is important to communicate how you feel about your partner's diabetes. Don't keep your feelings to yourself until you are ready to explode. Seek medical guidance or counseling if you think your situation is serious or if it is jeopardizing your relationship. You and your partner may decide to embrace conflict resolution techniques for couples or other communication techniques to help you both understand the other's perspective.

NICOLE

"It is really difficult to fight fair when in the middle of a blood sugar excursion (high or low). Personality is affected and that can mean lashing out or retreating. It is so important that my partner have knowledge of this and delicately approach it when necessary. There are times when I say things I don't mean and then regret those words later. It is hard to admit this kind of failure to the one I love the most. Remember, I don't like anything about living with diabetes and definitely feel self-conscious about how my diabetes affects relationships."

If your partner does not manage diabetes effectively, it is important to share your concerns with your partner. Without showing any sign of judgment or anger, you may offer to help in whatever way your partner wishes you to be involved. If your partner is in serious denial of diabetes, make sure you express your concern—and encourage your partner to seek medical and emotional guidance.

Bottom line, make sure your partner knows how much he/she means to you, how much you appreciate all that he/she goes through to live with diabetes, and how you wish to be supportive—whatever that looks like for you and your partner.

PARTNER ADVICE

Make an agreement to use a time-out during an argument if either of you suspects blood sugar may be high or low. Treat it if necessary and later return to the discussion.

CHAPTER THREE

―――――――― ❧ ――――――――

Managing Your Fear

LORRAINE

"Because type 1 diabetes is complex and unpredictable, severe medical emergencies that are both serious and scary are possible. As your partner ages, there are risks of diabetes-related complications including kidney disease, heart disease, stroke, nerve damage, amputations and impaired vision. All of these medical events may cause huge fear in you as a partner. I know from experience—throughout our marriage I bet I've spent a year's worth of time worrying about Chris—and helping him to survive!"

Fear is real and natural when living with a chronic life-threatening condition. It is important to identify when your fear is warranted and when your fear is irrational. If your partner is in good control of his/her diabetes, a severe medical emergency is less likely. You may consider creating a method of communication with your partner regarding his/her health. Some couples use CGM tools like the Dexcom SHARE to transmit blood glucose values. Others rely on a consistent phone call or text message when their partner is traveling and spending the night alone and away from home. Some partners listen for the blood sugar level sound indication of some meters to be cognizant of their loved ones blood sugar level when they are within earshot. Regardless of which system of communication you use, make sure to have a discussion with your partner about what kind of behavior from you is helpful and what is harmful.

PARTNER PERSPECTIVE

"The Dexcom CGM Share is a lifesaver. It allows me to remotely monitor my partner's glucose levels. The CGM alarms me when my partner goes below 55 so I can make sure he is capable of treating his hypoglycemia."

PARTNER OF SOMEONE WITH T1D

In a serious low blood sugar medical emergency where your partner is unconscious or nearly unconscious—and can't answer questions you ask, it is important to know how to use a drug called glucagon. Glucagon is a rescue drug and works by directing the liver to release stored sugar into the bloodstream. Even though administering glucagon may be scary, you can overcome your fear by practicing with expired glucagon kits. Use expired kits to practice mixing the powder and fluid, and then injecting the mixture into an orange or other object that is not your partner. There are also apps available from Eli Lilly on glucagon use.

PARTNER ADVICE

Learn to recognize the physical changes in your partner when having a low blood sugar. Blank stare? Sweating? Trouble formulating words? Inability to answer a question you have asked? Each person with T1D is different.

Bottom line, you can't hurt your partner by administering glucagon when he or she is low. You may need to call paramedics or other emergency personnel. Do not be afraid to call 9-1-1—their job is to help you.

PARTNER PERSPECTIVES

"Make sure you know what to do when your partner has a serious low blood sugar. You need to medically take care of your loved one when they are in crisis."

PARTNER OF SOMEONE WITH T1D

Diabetes education is the best medicine to treat your fears of diabetes. Consider joining your partner in a diabetes education class. Or, learn what you can online. Gaining knowledge will go a long way toward allowing you to help your partner and embrace your life together with diabetes.

PARTNER ADVICE

If your partner is using a CGM and often doesn't hear the device alarm at night, place the receiver in a glass tumbler or cup. When the receiver alarms, the sound will be amplified by the glass.

Most importantly, discuss your fears directly with your partner. A candid discussion with your partner may go a long way in helping you cope with life with diabetes, and it may even help create a stronger bond between you both.

PARTNER PERSPECTIVE

"I felt confident in my abilities to manage diabetes once I learned how to use my partner's insulin pump and CGM, and learned how to inject insulin and glucagon."

PARTNER OF SOMEONE WITH T1D

Emotional Elephants in the Room

NICOLE

*"We bet you are beginning to see a pattern in these chapters…open commu-
nication with your partner with diabetes is essential for a healthy relationship. It can be challenging to talk about the hard parts of life, but by doing
it you can reap so many rewards. My strongest relationships are with those
that have the sensitivity to understand my fears, the courage to talk through
those fears and the strength to encourage me to fight harder."*

Here is a given: 100 percent of people do not like having diabetes. Most partners
don't wish to burden anyone with their disease—especially not their signifi-
cant other. Often, the "burden" concern becomes a problem in the relationship.
The partner with diabetes may have guilt and shame—or have experienced real
or perceived stigma—for having to deal with this disease. All of these emotions
and experiences contribute to emotional distress and are something you should
be aware of. Take on this "elephant in the room" and make sure your partner
knows you support him/her through thick and thin—and that includes diabetes.

PARTNER ADVICE

Find ways to laugh about the diabetes blood sugar "roller coaster." Even though your partner may be trying hard to manage blood sugar, sometimes nothing seems to work. Having your support will help reduce stress and frustration.

People with diabetes worry about losing their partners, when often, you are the one petrified of losing your loved one due to their disease. Again, this "unspeakable" discussion should be addressed. By having this difficult discussion, you may strengthen your relationship. It is always important to be open, honest and real, and to strategize together how to best manage fears.

Another elephant to address: non-normal blood sugars, both low and high, and the way those blood sugars affect your partner's mood. These diabetes-induced mood swings are often difficult to tolerate. Talk with your partner about ways you can both survive the roller coaster of blood sugars and mood swings. It is likely your partner recognizes the mood swings, but feels helpless in handling them and regrets the way the mood swings affect relationships generally. Developing a code word to defuse situations is one strategy to try. Sometimes being silly can shake the situation enough to release the immediate stress.

PARTNER PERSPECTIVE

"We need to understand words and actions expressed during non-normal blood sugar periods are not from our partners— it is diabetes talking."

PARTNER OF SOMEONE WITH T1D

The next elephant is knowing when and when not to ask questions. In the situation of a low blood sugar episode, your partner may be embarrassed, especially if they have no memory of the situation. Even though you are anxious to discuss the episode, your partner may not wish to do so. Agree on guidelines for when and how you will discuss these types of delicate situations. Creating and respecting boundaries are important for relational health, especially with diabetes.

PARTNER ADVICE

Try to come up with other ways to say, "What's your blood sugar?" This phrase is not typically appreciated by people with T1D. It is often responded to with one word, "Fine."

Ask yourself if your curiosity is necessary in that moment. Are you about to exercise together? Is your partner with T1D about to take a road trip?

Perhaps you and your partner can come up with an honest way to address when sharing this information is important, and how to do so in a positive and productive way.

Ideas to try: Why not create new ways and environments to communicate with each other? Enjoy quality time in a natural setting like a park or beach. Talk about ways to strengthen your relationship generally, and address your diabetes challenges more specifically. By scheduling time for quality conversation, your ability to address the "elephants in the room" will be much easier for both you and your partner.

Don't underestimate the power of humor. Life was meant to be fun—why not laugh often about the trials and tribulations of diabetes?!

PARTNER PERSPECTIVE

"Make sure you laugh! My partner and I love sharing the story of a low blood sugar episode when the ice cream cone couldn't quite find my partner's mouth and instead was smeared all over his face. So funny!"

PARTNER OF SOMEONE WITH T1D

༄༅

Depression—Both Your Partner's and Yours

NICOLE

"Type 1 diabetes is tough—don't let anyone tell you otherwise. Individuals with T1D never get a break from diabetes and neither do our partners. It is exhausting and is never easy. Adding this physical and emotional burden to the one we love can leave the person with diabetes feeling much regret, and we likely never talk about the regret or guilt we feel."

Because the disease is so challenging to manage and so unpredictable, it is easy to get depressed. No matter how hard your partner might work to achieve good diabetes control, the results are often disappointing. Because there is so much we don't know about diabetes, it is important to remember that it is impossible to have perfect blood sugars all the time. Here is a way to think of it, diabetes can seem like a game where the rules constantly change without any explanation.

Research studies have shown there is a correlation between diabetes and depression. Encourage your partner to reach out to trained psychology professionals if they seem or are feeling depressed. The good news is: depression is a treatable condition.

With good news comes a little bit of bad news. Even though mental health research has advanced in the last two decades, depression often goes undiagnosed and untreated. It is important to recognize the symptoms, inquire about their duration and severity, and seek appropriate treatment.

NICOLE

"There have been times in my life that diabetes became overwhelming to the point of my ignoring it so I didn't have to deal with the frustration. In these times, help from a loving partner is so valued. You can often see what we can't see and can help us take action before we reach a breaking point."

According to the National Institute of Mental Health, symptoms of depression may include the following:

- Difficulty concentrating, remembering details, and making decisions

- Fatigue and decreased energy

- Feelings of guilt, worthlessness, and/or helplessness

- Feelings of hopelessness and/or pessimism

- Insomnia, early-morning wakefulness, or excessive sleeping

- Irritability, restlessness

- Loss of interest in activities or hobbies once pleasurable, including sex

- Overeating or appetite loss

- Persistent aches or pains, headaches, cramps, or digestive problems that do not ease even with treatment

- Persistent sad, anxious, or "empty" feelings

- Thoughts of suicide, suicide attempts

PARTNER PERSPECTIVE

"As my partner has aged, he has had to struggle with more diabetes complications. Over time, he has been more depressed. Meeting with trained medical professionals has helped. We are now looking at having an anti-depressant prescribed."

PARTNER OF SOMEONE WITH T1D

Even if your partner is not clinically depressed, he or she may experience "diabetes burnout." This is a state in which people with diabetes grow tired of managing the disease and choose to ignore it for a period of time. Thankfully, there are ways you can help your partner cope. Encourage your partner to accept "less than perfection" in his or her diabetes management. "Good enough" is fine for a short period of time. Even though tight blood sugar control will help minimize diabetes complications in the future, taking a short break from tight control won't cause complications overnight. Don't be afraid to encourage your partner to reach out to healthcare professionals, family and friends. Once your partner is in a better place and is less frustrated, a normal diabetes management routine may be resumed.

HOW DO YOU COPE AS A PARTNER?

You may also be feeling stress that is challenging to manage. To help you identify the causes of your stress and strategize solutions, the Diabetes Empowerment Foundation offers a free online tool to help you, the partner, with any diabetes-related frustrations and worries. The Partner Diabetes Distress Scale is designed to help you evaluate the amount and kind of diabetes-related distress you may be experiencing, what might be contributing to your distress, and tips to help you deal with it.

PARTNER ADVICE

The Partner Diabetes Distress Scale (PDDS) can help you understand your diabetes-related distress and provide tips to help you deal with it. *http://diabetespartners.org*

Even though you are focused on being a supportive partner, you must always remember to take care of yourself. Taking care of yourself may mean escaping from diabetes from time-to-time by empowering a close friend or loved one to check on your partner so you can enjoy "me" time.

LORRAINE

"Diabetes is hard on the individual who must live with the disease. What is much less discussed is the toll it takes on the partner. Over time, the fear of low blood sugars and complications, the challenge of tolerating diabetes-induced mood swings in your partner and your relationship's constant companion—diabetes—can wear you down."

PARTNER PERSPECTIVE

"Even though there are few chronic disease support groups for partners, I have received great encouragement from other partners of people with T1D, often with wine glasses in hand!"

PARTNER OF SOMEONE WITH T1D

You may also wish to learn stress relief practices such as meditation, deep breathing, yoga and exercise. These activities will help you reduce stress and boost your energy and mood. Invite your partner to join you and benefit from these activities as well!

PARTNER PERSPECTIVE

"Pray and be grateful for all of God's blessings bestowed upon you. That will help you cope as a partner."

PARTNER OF SOMEONE WITH T1D

CHAPTER SIX

How Involved Should You Be?

LORRAINE

"An important role for you as a partner is being an advocate for your loved one. When your partner is ill or impaired, it is obvious what role you must play. On the other hand, it is less obvious what role you should play with your partner's day-to-day diabetes management. I know my role in Chris' diabetes life is constantly changing, depending on his medical and emotional needs. And no day is ever the same."

Each relationship will be different. Some individuals with diabetes enjoy having their partner involved in all aspects of their diabetes life including medical appointments and daily care routines. Others prefer their partner be less involved. Once again, it comes down to communication. It is important for you to have a conversation with your partner to determine your appropriate amount of involvement. This conversation will help establish the optimal balance in your relationship.

PARTNER ADVICE

Make sure what you say is translated correctly by a partner with diabetes. Ask your partner to paraphrase what you said to make sure you are both on the same page. Incorrect interpretations often lead to conflict.

Because of the risks involved in managing this disease, it is common for the partner without diabetes to ask questions about their partner's blood sugar. Almost all relationships are strained by the nagging question, "What is your blood sugar?" If this question annoys your partner, it is important to talk through how this information is shared and in what environment it should and should not be asked. Perhaps your partner texts you every few hours to let you know he/she is OK. Perhaps your partner allows you to be alerted for low blood sugars through the SHARE feature on the Dexcom CGM. There are many ways to share information without putting either of you on the defensive or seeming parental to your partner.

PARTNER ADVICE

Get to know your partner's diabetes management team—endocrinologist or primary care physician, nurse practitioner, nurse educator, dietitian, etc. These professionals welcome partner participation and may be enormously helpful to you and your partner.

Another area to support your partner is to help stay on top of medical appointments, screenings and other recommendations. It can be confusing and overwhelming to schedule and remember all of the exams necessary to be healthy. Remember that each year people with diabetes should be screened for the signs of complications, including vision changes and foot health.

PARTNER PERSPECTIVE

"I attend my partner's medical appointments whenever I can—it brings us both peace of mind. I often help my partner prepare a list of questions/concerns to share at each appointment."

PARTNER OF SOMEONE WITH T1D

In the end, it is up to you and your partner to come up with the best way to support each of your needs. Communicating about each of your areas of concern will pave the way for greater understanding. It is likely that you are concerned about your partner's overall health and, specifically, low blood sugars that may be dangerous while your partner is concerned about being a burden to you. Through open communication, you can strike the best balance of involvement.

NICOLE

"This is a topic that can change over time with your T1D. There have been times in my life (like pregnancy) where I wanted a lot of partner involvement with my diabetes, but then other times where I did not.

At times I have removed my partner's access to my diabetes SHARE blood sugar data (Yes, you did just read that!) because my partner started to over analyze my diabetes information or used judgmental words to question my behavior or decisions. Once we resolved our communication issues I became more willing to share again.

Keeping the topic of diabetes engagement as an open topic will help. Most of all, I crave reassurance and support from my partner. I love to hear that you are proud of me or that you want to support my efforts to be healthy."

PARTNER PERSPECTIVE

"Realizing that under proper control, a person with diabetes can do ANYTHING but they never get a break from day-to-day management."

PARTNER OF SOMEONE WITH T1D

CHAPTER SEVEN

Diabetes Life Challenges

The daily grind of everyday life with diabetes can be overwhelming. There is so much for your partner to do and for you to know. In this section we create a list of diabetes topics and life events that are important for you to understand. This is not an exhaustive list, but it does provide information on the areas you will most often experience together.

ALCOHOL

Adults with diabetes are advised to drink alcohol in moderation. It is important to know that drinking alcohol can cause blood sugars to drop dangerously low. This occurs when the liver is so busy processing the excess alcohol (a toxin) that it can't produce glucose and protect your loved one when he/she is having a low blood sugar. When consuming alcohol, it is best to be more vigilant about blood sugar management.

Here are some tips related to alcohol and diabetes:

- Don't drink on an empty stomach

- Don't use extended or dual wave bolus for insulin when consuming alcohol or planning to consume alcohol

- Remember alcohol and exercise are not a good combination for a person with diabetes

- Check blood sugar often when drinking alcohol

- Always eat a bedtime snack after drinking alcohol

- Check blood sugar as soon as your loved one wakes up in the morning

BLOOD SUGAR CONTROL

The best ways to monitor blood sugar levels are through a blood glucose meter (or glucometer) and a continuous glucose monitor (CGM). Most insurance companies, including Medicare, cover these devices.

Your partner's target A1c goal may vary depending on age and other factors. What is generally recommended is an A1c level below 7.0%, which translates to an estimated average glucose of 154 mg/dL.

Blood sugar management is a delicate balance—there are no hard and fast rules for everyone to follow since everyone's diabetes behaves differently. When your partner's blood sugar is below 65 mg/dL, make sure that low blood sugar treatment is underway, or at least readily available. When your partner's blood sugar is above his/her target (or over 200 mg/dL) a combination of insulin delivery and exercise may be required.

If blood sugars are high for an extended period of time, often due to illness or an inadequate amount of injected insulin, the body will begin to burn fat for energy. This process produces ketones that may cause the blood to be acidic. High levels of ketones can poison the body and lead to diabetic ketoacidosis

(DKA), a serious condition that can result in a diabetic coma or even death. It is helpful to have ketone urine testing strips in your home at all times, and even a blood sugar meter that also has ketone testing capability. When ketones are present, your partner should not exercise.

CONFUSION ABOUT DIABETES

Soon after you enter into a relationship with your partner with diabetes, you will become knowledgeable about the challenges associated with this disease—including the general public's lack of understanding of type 1 diabetes, and the confusion between type 1 and type 2 diabetes. You may find yourself telling everyone you meet that type 1 diabetes is an autoimmune disorder and isn't caused by eating too many carbohydrates or sugar.

The best way to keep your cool is to take a deep breath—and then educate. Type 1 diabetes is similar to other autoimmune diseases such as rheumatoid arthritis, lupus, thyroid disease and inflammatory bowel disease. In each of these diseases, the body's immune system has confused "good" from "bad" and has, mistakenly, destroyed vitally important cells, such as the insulin-producing beta cells in the case of T1D.

COMPLICATIONS

Even though recent diabetes drugs and technology have significantly improved diabetes outcomes in most individuals with T1D, your partner may still have more sick days and hospitalizations than others. Over time, your partner may experience more disability issues. Long-term diabetes may cause medical complications such as heart, kidney and eye disease, or even limb amputations and stroke. Painful neuropathy symptoms due to nerve damage may occur especially at night.

People with diabetes are twice as likely to develop heart disease than someone without diabetes. Make sure the following tests are conducted with regularity: lipid profile (LDL, HDL, cholesterol, triglycerides) and for some, C-reactive protein.

People with T1D are also at greater risk for other autoimmune diseases such as thyroid disease, inflammatory bowel disease, rheumatoid arthritis, etc. It is important to have a general knowledge of these conditions and know how to identify warning signs that indicate a discussion is needed with your medical team.

Not only will you need to figure out how to best support your partner—both physically and emotionally, you will need to learn how you can cope with these often challenging complications. Finding others to support you during these difficult times is one way to cope. Stress relief activities such as meditation, exercise and prayer are other ways to cope. By making sure you take care of yourself, you will be more effective in providing strength and emotional support to your partner.

PARTNER PERSPECTIVE

"How does one cope with a lifelong partner with type 1 diabetes plus a cardiac condition, neuropathy, visual loss, mental haziness? To borrow from Nike, you 'just do it'!"

PARTNER OF SOMEONE WITH T1D

DISCRIMINATION

As your life with diabetes progresses, you will also begin to see how discrimination exists for those who have the disease. Because your partner may worry about employer discrimination and job security (even though there are legal protections in place), they may choose not to publicly disclose their diabetes in the workplace. Even Hollywood actors and professional athletes with diabetes, among people in numerous other professions, have shared that discrimination related to the disease has negatively impacted their careers.

EXERCISE

Exercise is a critical component of good diabetes management. One way to be supportive of your partner is to exercise with him or her. Walking or light movement will do loads of good for your loved one's diabetes management. Keep in mind that anaerobic exercise (lifting weights; resistance exercises) causes less initial decline in blood sugar during the activity, while aerobic exercise (running, walking) often has an immediate effect on blood sugar. Your partner may need to adjust plans for activity depending on their blood sugar at the time. Some intense exercises can cause blood sugar levels to rise. If this is the case, discuss strategies to manage the rise in blood sugar with a health professional to allow you and your loved one to still enjoy the activities you desire.

PARTNER PERSPECTIVE

"My partner and I enjoy taking walks together after meals, it is a time to connect and it helps manage post-meal blood sugar spikes."

PARTNER OF A T1D

FOOD

To manage diabetes, your partner must carefully monitor food intake and activity to dose insulin correctly. Your partner may eat almost anything—as long as the food is balanced with insulin and activity.

By counting carbohydrates, your partner may effectively manage this delicate balance of food + exercise + insulin. Since food is such a big part of any relationship, it may be helpful if you learn how to count carbohydrates. A certified diabetes educator can be a valuable resource in learning about diabetes nutrition recommendations and food management.

PARTNER ADVICE

Helpful consumer tools include the Calorie King books, *www.calorieking.com*, or any of the fitness apps such as My Fitness Pal, *www.myfitnesspal.com* or Fitbit, *www.fitbit.com*.

Diabetes myths abound. Most people assume T1Ds can't eat any type of sugar. This is not true. As long as carbs or sugars are accounted for, they may be included in your partner's diet. You and your partner may consider meeting with a trained nutritionist to discuss myths and truths about diet, and to secure menu-planning ideas for your family.

PARTNER PERSPECTIVE

"Our life changed for the better when my partner went on the pump. We didn't have to eat at a set time every day and have been able to enjoy meals together."

PARTNER OF SOMEONE WITH T1D

It is important to educate your family and friends on the dietary needs of your partner, especially during holiday meals and special gatherings. Even though your partner may eat anything, the more carbs consumed, the more insulin will be required. High doses of insulin may cause weight gain and other health challenges.

INSULIN

There are numerous types of insulin on the market and they all work differently. Some are short-acting; some are long-acting. Insulin therapy that controls blood sugar levels when you eat is called fast-acting or bolus insulin. Insulin therapy that controls blood sugar levels between meals and during sleep is called long-acting or basal insulin.

LOW BLOOD SUGAR EPISODES (HYPOGLYCEMIA)

Sugar is found everywhere and is the antidote for hypoglycemia (low blood sugar). In a low blood sugar situation, diet or sugar free foods are not useful. Also, foods with considerable fat, such as candy bars, may take longer to elevate the low blood sugar than juice, fruit snacks, or other emergency foods that do not have fat.

For a severe low blood sugar that results in lack of consciousness or seizures, glucagon should be administered. Glucagon tutorials may be found online.

PREGNANCY AND CHILDREN

As you and partner travel down the road called life, there are other choices to be made such as having children. Your partner may be worried about the risks for passing T1D to your children. The risk for a child developing diabetes is lower if it is the mother—rather than the father—who has T1D. If the father has T1D, the risk is approximately 10 percent. If the mother has T1D and gives birth before age 25, the risk is 4 percent. If the mother is over age 25 when giving birth, the risk is 1 percent.

PARTNER PERSPECTIVE

"Pregnancy was one of the scariest times of our lives. She was incredible with how she managed her diabetes, but we were both scared the entire time."

PARTNER OF SOMEONE WITH T1D

For women with diabetes who wish to have children, there are a host of issues to be addressed before and during pregnancy. Fertility may be an issue, especially if the woman is not in tight diabetes control. Getting early and regular prenatal care that mandates tight blood sugar control will improve the chances of an uncomplicated pregnancy, a smooth delivery, and a healthy mother and child.

PARTNER ADVICE

We encourage you to check out this Moms with Diabetes webpage: *https://www.diabetesempowerment.org/moms-with-diabetes*. This resource provides a look at a couple grappling with the decisions and the experience of pregnancy with diabetes—together.

You or your partner may be concerned about the possibility of having hypoglycemia (low blood sugar) episodes when caring for your children. With today's improved diabetes management tools including the CGM, these fears may be alleviated or at least minimized. As stated earlier in this book, open communication about concerns and careful planning will help calm fears and help everyone feel more comfortable.

TRAVEL

Diabetes never takes a vacation so, unfortunately, travel may be more difficult for you and your partner. Allow for more time at airport security checkpoints since insulin pumps, blood sugar meters, CGMs, insulin, syringes, insulin pens, and medications often rattle cautious airport security personnel. Even though you will be told X-rays will not denature insulin, there are many different types of insulin today so you can ask for a visual inspection.

Time differences encountered while traveling can cause challenges for your partner's diabetes management. Don't be surprised if unexpected low or high blood sugars occur while traveling. (You may wish to gently remind your partner to change insulin pump settings to reflect new time zones and to check blood sugar levels more frequently when in a new environment.)

PARTNER ADVICE

Make sure you and your partner carry an updated list of drugs/devices—and a list of doctors with contact information when you travel.

If you are traveling internationally, recognize every country's medical system is different. Expect to encounter high costs and/or a different standard of care and different diabetes drugs, devices and medical care. Bring backup supplies and medications, and even backup pumps and blood glucose meters—just in case your technology fails or your travel is delayed. Bring lots of emergency food for low blood sugars. Also consider having copies of prescriptions with you in case you need to purchase items during your trip. You may also want to purchase medical travel insurance in advance of your trip to be on the safe side.

Even at home, traveling by car may be a challenge. It's important for people to know what their blood sugar is before getting behind the wheel. Stock your car with low blood sugar supplies, such as glucose tablets, juice boxes, and fruit snacks. Encourage your partner to stay in touch with you so you don't worry. Remember, insulin is fragile and the potency can be affected by heat exposure. Don't leave diabetes supplies in a hot car.

Encourage your partner to consider wearing a diabetes medical alert necklace, bracelet or other identification. In case of a medical emergency, this medical identification may save your partner's life. There are many fashionable designs available for both men and women.

PARTNER PERSPECTIVE

"Learn as much as you can so you can be the best support possible. However, don't ever act like you're an expert. You may know a lot but you will never really know what it is like to deal with diabetes 24/7."

PARTNER OF SOMEONE WITH T1D

YOUR GOLDEN YEARS

As you and your partner reach your "autumn of life," you will both experience the usual issues involving aging. Diabetes may accelerate the aging process in some people. Your role may need to change as your partner's diabetes needs change. There may be more medical visits, greater frustrations with insurance companies and Medicare, eyesight issues that cause challenges with medication delivery and technology operation, and an increased fear of disability and death. Your partner may also experience balance issues and may be more susceptible to falls, and strokes. Because your partner's ability to sense low blood sugar may decrease or disappear, a CGM may be highly recommended and will help ease your concerns.

As people age, personalities often change for both partners. Even though your loved one may have been mild-mannered throughout life and managed diabetes well, as an older adult he or she may have a more negative disposition and become easily confused about their diabetes. Your partner may be less able to count carbs, plan meals, monitor blood sugar levels and determine correct insulin doses.

As a partner, you may become less patient and supportive, even though you are still very much in love with your partner. You may also need to focus on your own health issues versus that of your partner.

If aging is causing you or your partner great challenges—especially as it relates to diabetes management, you may ask your physician for guidance and support. Perhaps a referral to a geriatrician or another aging specialist would be helpful, or even in-home elder care support.

If you find yourself fearful or anxious about losing your partner, reach out to someone and talk about your feelings. This is a challenging part of life. To help you cope, make sure you enjoy the time you have with your partner. Create special memories. Write down these memories—or even your fears—in a journal. And if your anxiety becomes too much to handle, seek a good therapist or grief counselor. Don't try to go it alone.

Even though aging has challenges that are made more difficult by diabetes, both partners will benefit from a loving relationship, open communication, and the willingness to ask for help when needed.

PARTNER PERSPECTIVE

"No one enjoys the aging process. Aging with diabetes is exceptionally hard. After experiencing very difficult complications including multiple strokes, my partner and I constantly remind ourselves that 'every day is a gift' and we live each day like it is our last together."

PARTNER OF SOMEONE WITH T1D

CHAPTER 8

Diabetes Between the Sheets

Sexual intimacy helps to keep a relationship healthy and strong. Unfortunately, type 1 diabetes can create multiple challenges in this department. The key is planning ahead. For instance, since low blood sugar may occur during sex, it is good to have juice boxes and glucose tablets nearby. For insulin pump placement challenges, decide if there is a particular piece of clothing to hold your partner's pump, or if it is best to detach the pump during sex. There are sexy ways to wear or handle your diabetes devices, you just have to be creative.

PARTNER PERSPECTIVE

"Be a good listener and be empathetic before and during intimate times."

PARTNER OF A T1D

With uncontrolled and/or long-term type 1 diabetes, sexual performance can be difficult. Sexual performance issues in diabetes can be linked to elevated blood sugar over time, which damages nerves and blood vessels.

Erectile dysfunction and delays in satisfaction may be a problem for men with diabetes. There are numerous treatment options now on the market including oral medications, suppositories, injections, vacuum pumps, and penile implants. Encourage your partner to try one or more of these options to find the one that works best for both of you.

For women with diabetes, vaginal dryness can be an issue and therefore it is important to lubricate during intimate times. By the way, make sure her lubricant is sugar-free. Yes, read the label. ☺ Lubrication will help your partner enjoy intimacy and will lessen potential painful experiences for her.

Women with diabetes must also consider that sex can lead to an increase in yeast infections. This is more common in women with diabetes than those without diabetes. Higher blood sugar levels before and during sex can increase the likelihood for infection.

Even with the vast number of options available today to enhance performance, these drugs/devices may not always work. With the constant juggling of pills and gadgets, your relationship may suffer. Recognize that sexual spontaneity may be limited.

Once again, open communication is the best way to handle these diabetes sexual challenges. Don't be afraid to engage medical professionals and therapists to help you and your partner. A competent urologist can be helpful to both men and women with diabetes—and may end up being your best support system for your time between the sheets.

PARTNER PERSPECTIVE

"Be creative in the bedroom. Role-playing, adult games and videos help my partner and I enjoy a great sex life, even though my partner's diabetes doesn't always cooperate."

PARTNER OF SOMEONE WITH T1D

·❦·

The T1D Partner Perspective

To help you better understand your own partner with diabetes, we share two T1D partner stories with you.

CHRIS STIEHL, T1D SINCE 1960

"Normal relationships are often very complicated. Having a relationship with someone who has a chronic disease such as T1D is even more complicated. As a person with T1D, I worry about so many things: What is my blood sugar? Which way is it heading? How rapidly? What food is being digested in my stomach? How rapidly will the carbohydrates be absorbed? Is my insulin pump working properly? Is the site of the infusion set infected? What about my CGM? Has it been calibrated? How well are the pump infusion site and CGM site adhering to my skin? Do I have supplies—medications, syringes, pump parts—handy? These worries make relationship management with a partner difficult at best.

When my blood sugars are elevated, my personality changes and I am easily angered. My partner needs to be able to understand that fact. I sometimes ask her to stay away from me until I get in a better blood sugar range. At times, she will ask me what my blood sugar is in the middle of an argument. This angers me, as I feel as though my blood sugar has nothing to do with the fight. Often, she is correct and my blood sugar is elevated. We then call a time out until I am in a better range, then we resume the discussion, if needed.

At times asking for help from your partner is difficult, especially if you are an independent person. Be sure to let your partner know how to help and not to fear helping you. Some people feel that asking for assistance may be viewed as a sign of weakness. The person with T1D needs to understand that receiving kindness and love from their partner is not a sign of weakness, but a sign of the strength of the relationship. Learning to ask for and to accept help from your partner can be an enormous hurdle. Once this barrier has been cleared, it can add significantly to the trust and degree of partnership, as well as the partner's understanding of your disease.

Dealing with the reality of type 1 diabetes may lead to friction and challenges. And yet, partners facing these difficulties together can discover unanticipated but equally intimate and rewarding moments. Caring for someone with T1D can lead to frustrations. The disease can be treated the same way in identical situations with drastically different outcomes on successive days. Patience, communication and networking with other partners of those with T1D can help avoid partner burnout.

In my opinion, the key to a successful partnership is letting the other person know what your needs are and how they can best meet those needs."

NICOLE JOHNSON, T1D SINCE 1993

"Relationships are not easy! They involve work, negotiation, and understanding. When we get it right, relationships are the fragrance of life and they provide immense joy. The balance between independence and dependence in relationships is probably what confounds the diabetes experience so much. Individuals with diabetes often consider how to share about our diabetes, but not completely share—me included. We all tend to worry about not scaring our partner off, but at the same time crave the special understanding and reassurance that can only come from a partner.

People with T1D fight to be seen as capable and strong, while on the inside we struggle with feeling broken and weak. That doesn't mean we feel limited, but the small moments of frustration add up and can cause unseen emotional damage. Every day I have a moment or two that I look at my sensor or my pump with disdain. "Why me?" crosses my mind. I then have a brief moment of hatred of the device- of my reality. I have learned how to snap myself back to thankfulness quickly though.

In relationships, I have found myself disclosing diabetes at the beginning and then expecting sensitive care. If the sensitivity is not present, the relationship does not progress. I can't handle terse or harsh responses related to my most personal struggle and the root of much of my own self-doubt [diabetes].

I also can't handle overbearing and intense responses. Anyone who makes my private battle a public ordeal (in a way that I am not making it an ordeal) does not have staying power either. It is a challenge to find an individual with the emotional intelligence to wade through the muck of physical and emotional diabetes realities.

What I want most from my partner is a sweetness in approach to my disease. ☺ It cannot be his disease. I do not want him to "own" it, but I want partnership in approach toward it. I don't need instructive guidance on how to best care for myself, I need a supportive person that will listen to my frustrations and use humor to help me get to acceptance. Together we can conquer the challenge, the trick is in negotiating how we will get there.

My perceptions of judgment are challenging. I need my partner to remember that I judge myself for my own imperfection and diabetes failures on a daily basis. If you pile more judgment on top of that it becomes more than I can bear. I need you to deflect and defuse my own self-doubt or destructive behaviors. For example, asking me to go for a walk will go much further than asking why my blood sugar was high. Conversely, if I have a low blood sugar, don't talk or ask—act. Sweetness and sensitivity are important here again. Don't overdo it; don't call attention to me when I am weak. Don't make me feel broken. Help me repair and regain my composure so we can move forward together. I remember one person in my life responded to a low blood sugar by anxiously moving around a room gathering cookies and sweets. I was horribly embarrassed. While that person was anxiously finding things to use to help me, a completely unrelated person passed me a hard candy and helped me far more. That quiet person made me feel like I could make it through the situation, not like I was the situation. This is such an important distinction.

Joining in the fight against diabetes can be a great connector and so meaningful to your partners. It can be anything from going to a diabetes gala together or walking in a fundraising walk. Small ways that show you feel your partner is strong and brave help your partner with diabetes feel more confident in sharing the struggle."

CHAPTER 10

Diabetes Can Empower You

Even though diabetes is not fun for you or your partner, good things may happen as you take this journey together.

PARTNER PERSPECTIVE

"You and your partner are a team that can surmount the insurmountable. Don't ever think otherwise, and don't ever live otherwise."

PARTNER OF SOMEONE WITH T1D

Throughout this book we've shared that communication is key to relationship success. Since there are so many issues involved with this disease, the most successful couples figure out how to best communicate and support each other. Through diabetes, you may end up creating a deeper, more meaningful connection with your partner.

PARTNER PERSPECTIVE

"Our motto is we play the hand God gave us."

PARTNER OF SOMEONE WITH T1D

When you have a partner with diabetes who is focused on eating balanced meals, exercising and managing stress, you may join in and find your own health improves.

Don't forget the healing power of humor. Diabetes is often so challenging, so utterly unpredictable that you just have to laugh when things don't go right. Research suggests daily laughter helps to improve overall health and may even help to lower blood sugar. Laughter stimulates positive emotions and helps you and your partner cope with the daily challenges of this disease. Let the giggling, chuckling and deep belly laughter begin!

PARTNER ADVICE

Open communication, empathy, and a sprinkling of humor are the magic ingredients for you and your partner to survive diabetes.

Even though diabetes is a 24/7 disease, it doesn't have to take over your relationship in a negative way. It can actually improve your relationship and deepen the bond with your partner.

LORRAINE

"Living with a man with type 1 diabetes has been a tremendous opportunity. I've learned so much about the disease and have met so many people along the way. I am grateful for every day with this man. Together, we are surviving his diabetes, and becoming stronger."

REFERENCES

1. August, K. J., & Sorkin, D. H. (2010). Marital status and gender differences in managing a chronic illness: The function of health-related social control. Social Science & Medicine, 71, 1831–1838.

2. Beverly, E. A., Miller, C. K., & Wray, L. A. (2008). Spousal support and food-related behavior change middle-aged and older adults living with type 2 diabetes. Health Education & Behavior, 35, 707–720.

3. Trief, P.M., Ploutz-Snyder, R., Britton, K.D. et al. (2004). The relationship between marital quality and adherence to the diabetes care regimen. Annals of Behavioral Medicine, 27, 148–154.

4. Franks, M. M., Sahin, Z. S., Seidel, A. J., Shields, C. G., Oates, S. K., & Boushey, C. J. (2012). Table for two: Diabetes distress and diet-related interactions of married patients with diabetes and their spouses. Families, Systems, & Health, 30(2), 154–165.

5. August, K.J., Rook, K.S., Parris Stephens, M.A., et al. (2011). Are spouses of chronically ill partners burdened by exerting health-related social control? Journal of Health Psychology, 16, 1109–1119.

6. House, J. S., Umberson, D., & Landis, K. R. (1988). Structures and processes of social support. Annual Review of Sociology, 14(1), 293–318.

7. Bailey, B., & Kahn, A. (1993). Apportioning illness management authority: how diabetic individuals evaluate and respond to spousal help. Qualitative Health Research, 3(1), 55–73.

8. Trief, P. M., Sandberg, J., Greenberg, R. P., Graff, K., Castronova, N., Yoon, M., & Weinstock, R. S. (2003). Describing support: A qualitative study of couples living with diabetes. Families, Systems, & Health, 21(1), 57–67.

9. Johnson, N., & Melton, S. (2015). Partner Perspectives on Life with a Person with Type 1 Diabetes. PLAID-People Living with And Inspired by Diabetes, 1(2).

10. Franks, M. M., Lucas, T., Stephens, M. A. P., Rook, K. S., & Gonzalez, R. (2010). Diabetes distress and depressive symptoms: A dyadic investigation of older patients and their spouses. Family Relations, 59(5), 599–610.

11. August, K. J., Rook, K. S., Franks, M. M., & Parris Stephens, M. A. (2013). Spouses' involvement in their partners' diabetes management: Associations with spouse stress and perceived marital quality. Journal Of Family Psychology, 27(5), 712–721.

12. Miller, D., & Brown, J. L. (2005). Marital interactions in the process of dietary change for type 2 diabetes. Journal of Nutrition Education and Behavior, 37(5), 226–234.

13. Fisher, L., Polonsky, W. H., Hessler, D. M., Masharani, U., Blumer, I., Peters, A. L.,... & Bowyer, V. (2015). Understanding the sources of diabetes distress in adults with type 1 diabetes. Journal of Diabetes and its Complications, 29(4), 572–577.

14. Frederick, L., Cox, D., Kovatchev, B., Julian, D., & Clarke, W. (1997). The psychosocial impact of severe hypoglycemic episodes on spouses of patients with IDDM. Diabetes Care, 20(10), 1543–1546.

15. Ritholz, M. D., Beste, M., Edwards, S. S., Beverly, E. A., Atakov-Castillo, A., & Wolpert, H. A. (2014). Impact of continuous glucose monitoring on diabetes management and marital relationships of adults with Type 1 diabetes and their spouses: a qualitative study. Diabetic Medicine, (1), 47.

16. Trief, P.M., Wade, M.J., Britton, K.D. et al. (2002). Prospective analysis of marital relationship factors and quality of life in diabetes. Diabetes Care, 25, 1154–1158.

17. Rook, K. S. (2001). Emotional health and positive versus negative social exchanges: A daily diary analysis. Applied Developmental Science, 5(2), 86–97.

18. Centers for Disease Control. (2014). 2014 National Diabetes Statistics Report. https://www.cdc.gov/diabetes/pdfs/data/2014-report-estimates-of-diabetes-and-its-burden-in-the-united-states.pdf

19. Gottman, J., Gottman, J. M., & Silver, N. (1995). Why marriages succeed or fail: And how you can make yours last. Simon and Schuster.

Helpful Diabetes Organizations and Resources

AMERICAN DIABETES ASSOCIATION
www.diabetes.org

BEHAVIORAL DIABETES INSTITUTE
www.behavioraldiabetes.org

CLINICAL TRIALS
www.clinicaltrials.gov

DEXCOM
www.dexcom.com

DIABETES DAILY
www.diabetesdaily.com

DIABETES EMPOWERMENT FOUNDATION
www.diabetesempowerment.org

DIABETES HANDS FOUNDATION
www.diabeteshands.org

DIABETES MINE
www.diabetesmine.com

DIABETES ONLINE COMMUNITY AND BLOGGERS
https://diabetesadvocates.org/getting-to-know-the-diabetes-online-community-doc-2/

ELI LILLY GLUCAGON APP
http://www.lillyglucagon.com/#tools

JUVENILE DIABETES RESEARCH FOUNDATION
www.jdrf.org

MEDICALERT FOUNDATION
www.medicalert.org

THE DIATRIBE FOUNDATION
www.diaTribe.org

TAKING CONTROL OF YOUR DIABETES
www.tcoyd.org

BETA CELL The type of cell in the pancreas that makes insulin.

CARBOHYDRATE A class of food and a source of energy. Carbohydrates are mainly sugars and starches that the body breaks down into glucose.

CERTIFIED DIABETES EDUCATOR A health care professional who is certified by the American Association of Diabetes Educators to teach people with diabetes how to manage their condition.

DIABETES Diabetes is a disease in which the body's ability to produce or respond to the hormone insulin is impaired. The result is abnormal levels of glucose in the blood and urine.

GLUCAGON A hormone that raises the level of glucose in the blood by releasing stored glucose from the liver. This is sometimes injected into people with diabetes during a severe low blood sugar episode.

GLUCOSE This is a simple sugar that is an important energy source for living organisms. Glucose circulates in the blood stream.

HYPOGLYCEMIA This is when blood sugar or glucose drops below normal levels.

HYPERGLYCEMIA This is when blood sugar or glucose rises above recommended levels.

KETOACIDOSIS This is a serious condition that occurs when the body produces high levels of blood acids called ketones. This condition occurs when the body does not have enough insulin.

UROLOGIST A doctor who specializes in treatment of the urinary tract for men and women, as well as treatment of the genital organs for men.

ACKNOWLEDGMENTS

LORRAINE

I have so much to be thankful for including friends who have supported me over the years. One friend who is also a partner of someone with T1D, Ashley Wendel, strategized with me years ago about writing a book for partners. Two other friends and partners of loved ones with T1D, Karen Brownlee and Michele Huie, offered great support to this project in so many ways. And most importantly, a truly inspirational friend and diabetes colleague, Nicole Johnson, helped to make this partner book a reality.

We are so grateful to all of the partners who contributed their thoughts and quotes to this project. Your candid, heartfelt input is so appreciated. Your stories inspire us all!

NICOLE

I too am filled with gratitude. The opportunity to work with my colleagues Lorraine, Stephanie, Chris and John on this book is a gift. Their talents are a blessing to me and the diabetes community. I am also so honored to have been able to write with reflection on past relationship failures and future relationship success. Partners are so very important!

Nicole Johnson, DrPH, MPH, MA has worked in diabetes for over 20 years. She is most well known for her time as Miss America 1999. Nicole gained a reputation for her engagement in diabetes research focused on quality of life, psychosocial issues, and family dynamics during her time as the Executive Director of Bringing Science Home, a $7 million diabetes research program at the University of South Florida. Nicole's expertise in public health and social marketing allowed her to create and lead CDC funded statewide initiatives in Florida to expand access and acceptance of pre-diabetes and infant mortality education.

Nicole is a well-known public speaker and travels worldwide teaching about diabetes though her foundation. She also works in the non-profit world to create community based solutions to gaps in care for adults with Type 1 diabetes. Examples of programs she created include: Students With Diabetes, Diabetes Partners and Moms With Diabetes.

Over the years, Nicole has served on many diabetes advisory boards including the Florida Governor's Diabetes Advisory Council, the NIH Council of Public Representatives and the national boards for both the American Diabetes Association and JDRF.

In her journalism career, Nicole won a Telly Award for her work on the CNBC talk show dLife. Her love of journalism lead her to be a columnist for numerous diabetes magazines over the years, as well as the author of 8 books related to diabetes.

Lorraine Stiehl has been a diabetes partner and patient advocate for over 30 years. Together with her husband who has had type 1 diabetes for nearly six decades, they have survived and thrived with this chronic disease and its complications.

Lorraine has been active with JDRF since 1987. As a local, regional and national staff member for 14 years, she launched 17 chapters in 13 states and raised millions of dollars to support diabetes research. As a volunteer leader, she served as national chair for grassroots advocacy and chaired the national advocacy committee on the international board of directors. Lorraine was named 1992 national staff member of the year and 2010 national volunteer of the year.

Lorraine helped to create the University of California, San Francisco Diabetes Center, partnering with its renowned diabetes researchers and clinicians for 13 years. Through her family's consulting firm, StiehlWorks, Lorraine has provided marketing, communications, and development leadership to The diaTribe Foundation, Diabetes Hands Foundation, Diabetes Research Connection, Diabetes Empowerment Foundation, Students With Diabetes, Lymphoma Research Foundation, and the California Institute for Regenerative Medicine.

To support her passion for medical research and patient health, Lorraine recruits for clinical trials including Type 1 Diabetes TrialNet, and advocates for diabetes regulatory, reimbursement and access issues in partnership with the Washington DC-based public policy and advocacy firm, HCM Strategists.

Made in the USA
San Bernardino, CA
16 May 2018